KU-394-351

This star map has the South Celestial Pole as its centre. It shows constellations of the southern sky. Constellations lying across the celestial equator appear on both maps. Paler areas represent the Milky Way.

Constellations on the map of the southern sky featured in this book:

Carina – the Keel

Centaurus

Ophiuchus

Orion

Puppis – the Stern

Vela – the Sail

Note: Astronomers have divided the very large old constellation Argo into Carina (the Keel), Puppis (the Stern) and Vela (the Sail)

*TriA=Triangulum Australe
+ marks the Celestial Pole

FOR SIMON – J.M.
FOR MY SISTERS AMIRA AND DANNI – C.B.

PUBLIC LIBRARY
-46682
650873   SCH
J 523.8

Once Upon a Starry Night copyright © Frances Lincoln Limited 2003
Text copyright © Jacqueline Mitton 2003
Illustrations copyright © Christina Balit 2003

First published in Great Britain in 2003 by
Frances Lincoln Limited, 4 Torriano Mews
Torriano Avenue, London NW5 2RZ
www.franceslincoln.com

All rights reserved

No part of this publication may be reproduced, stored in a retrieval
system, or transmitted, in any form, or by any means, electrical,
mechanical, photocopying, recording or otherwise without
the prior written permission of the publisher or a licence
permitting restricted copying. In the United Kingdom
such licences are issued by the Copyright Licensing Agency,
90 Tottenham Court Road, London W1P 9HE.

British Library Cataloguing in Publication Data
available on request

ISBN 0-7112-2106-5

Printed in Hong Kong
9 8 7 6 5 4 3 2 1

ONCE UPON A STARRY NIGHT

Heroes and Gods of the Constellations

Jacqueline Mitton

Christina Balit

FRANCES LINCOLN

Schools Library and Information Services

S00000650873

THE LAST HINTS of pink and orange have faded in the west. Darkness creeps across the clear sky like a velvet curtain. It's a perfect night for telling a story.

But what about some pictures to go with the story? Look up, and what do you see? Not just stars, but a vast picture-book. The night sky is a realm of kings and queens, gods, heroes and mystical creatures. Look – they're all there, outlined by the stars. You only need a little imagination . . .

CASSIOPEIA

Where the Milky Way tumbles through the northern sky sits Queen Cassiopeia, a zigzag of dazzling stars, with Cepheus her king close by.

"See how beautiful I am," she declared one day, "fairer than all the nymphs of the sea."

Poseidon was angry with Cassiopeia. "No mortal insults my nymphs!" said the ocean god. "I'll punish you for your vanity." And he sent a frightful sea monster to terrify the kingdom.

ANDROMEDA

Andromeda is King Cepheus' beloved daughter. A spiral galaxy lies just beside her and the blue and yellow gem of a double star flashes on her skirt.

"Sacrifice your daughter – it's the only way to stop the beast," her father was told. So the princess was chained to rocks by the sea to await her horrible fate.

Her heart beat fast with fear. Would anyone help her before it was too late?

PERSEUS

Perseus to the rescue! Winged sandals on his feet, the hero speeds through the Milky Way to Andromeda's side. He carries the fearsome head of Medusa, the ghastly Gorgon he has slain. The Demon Star that is Medusa's eye winks eerily. Perseus holds high his magic sickle, twin star clusters glistening beside his hand.

"Death to the sea monster!" he cries.

So Andromeda was saved and bold Perseus married his princess.

PEGASUS

Pegasus the heavenly horse soars gracefully overhead, four bright stars at the corners of his Great Square.

After Perseus had killed Medusa, Pegasus sprang up where her blood had fallen. Faithfully the winged horse served the mighty god Zeus, carrying his thunder and lightning.

When the mortal Bellopheron mounted Pegasus and tried to ride him to the realm of the gods, angry Zeus flung him back to earth – but rewarded Pegasus for his loyal service by setting him in the stars.

LYRA

High in the sky, a great bird bears the lyre of Orpheus, adorned with bright stars and a wispy ring of gleaming gas.

Orpheus' singing left his listeners spellbound and the music of his lyre held them like a charm.

Grief-stricken after his young wife died, he softened the hearts of the underworld gods with his music.

"Your wife may follow you to the land of the living," they decreed, "so long as you do not look at her on the way." But Orpheus couldn't resist glancing back – and she was gone for ever.

HERCULES

Immortalised by the gods, Hercules the superhero kneels in the sky, a clustering ball of stars at his thigh.

Renowned for his many feats of strength, Hercules (called Herakles by the Ancient Greeks) could not be harmed by sword or fire because of the miraculous lion-skin he wore. He didn't fear the fiery dragon who guarded the golden apples of the Hesperides. For one of his famous labours he seized the apples – and crushed the dragon with his foot!

ORION

Striding boldly through the heavens comes the brilliant hunter Orion.

Son of the sea-god Poseidon, he could walk on water and was tall enough to wade through the ocean. So great a huntsman was this handsome giant, even the goddess Artemis deigned to hunt with him. But when he dared to touch her, Artemis was furious and her punishment speedy: Orion died from a scorpion's sting.

Now starry pearls stud his belt and where his sword hangs, a haze of glowing gas glistens.

CENTAURUS

Chiron the Centaur – half-man, half-horse – trots along the Milky Way.

Clever and kind, wise and fair, immortal Chiron was a wonderful teacher and healer. Then by chance a poisoned arrow struck him, and there was no cure.

"This pain is too great to bear for ever," he cried. He begged to die, and Zeus granted his wish, giving him an honoured place in the sky.

Now a fuzzy swarm of a million stars rides on the Centaur's back. Our nearest bright star, Alpha Centauri, burns yellow at his foot.

OPHIUCHUS

Is it dangerous to hold a snake? "I'm not afraid. This snake has healing powers," says the Serpent-holder Ophiuchus. This heavenly figure is the god of medicine whom the Ancient Greeks called Asclepius.

With his magical skills, Asclepius could even bring the dead back to life – but this made Zeus frown.

"No god should meddle with life and death in the world of mortals," he cried. Raising his thunderbolt, the king of the gods struck Asclepius down, but afterwards placed him among the stars.

ARGO

"**B**ring me the sacred golden fleece!" commanded Jason's scheming uncle (secretly thinking, "He'll die if he tries"). But undeterred, Jason and fifty friends set off in the great ship *Argo* on their dangerous adventure.

"To win the Fleece, first yoke my fiery bulls and sow these dragon's teeth," demanded the king who owned the Fleece. "Then fight the soldiers who spring up where the teeth fall." Impossible? No! With magical help, Jason won the Fleece.

Now the *Argo* sails a sea of stars as three constellations: keel, stern and sail.

Stars, nebulas and galaxies

The stars are like our Sun: huge balls of glowing gas. They look like small specks of light only because they are very far away. Some of the specks we see shining in the night sky look fuzzy. They are often called 'nebulas' – from the Latin word for clouds. But there are several different kinds of fuzzy objects. Some really are bright clouds of gas; others are families of stars. You can tell the difference when you look at them through a telescope.

We are in a galaxy of thousands of millions of stars: all the stars we see at night belong to it. The Milky Way is the light of many distant stars. Our galaxy is shaped like a disc with a bulge in the middle and spiral arms winding out from the bulge. It is a great island of stars in space and just one of billions of galaxies in the universe.

Constellations

The stars in a constellation look near to each other in the sky, but they are not really close together: they are scattered in space, all at different distances from us. When we say that a star is "in a constellation", it tells us where to find it on the sky, not where it is in space.

The whole sky is divided up between 88 different-sized constellations, just as a continent is divided into countries or states. Every star, star cluster, nebula or galaxy belongs to one of the constellations.

The official names of constellations are in Latin, though some of their names come from characters in Greek myths. This book uses the Greek names for the gods and goddesses who appear in the stories.

More about some night sky objects in this book

ANDROMEDA

The spiral galaxy in Andromeda is the most distant thing you can see without a telescope and the nearest large galaxy to our own. It is more than 2 million light years away, which means that the light we pick up from it now set out from the galaxy over 2 million years ago. Our Milky Way Galaxy is similar to the Andromeda galaxy, but not quite as large.

PERSEUS

The second brightest star in Perseus is called Algol or the Demon Star. Regular as clockwork, every 2 days 20 hours and 49 minutes it dims noticeably, then brightens again. In reality, Algol is a pair of stars going around each other. Normally we see their combined light, but when the fainter star crosses in front of the brighter one, it cuts out some of the light, and the pair looks fainter.

In Perseus you can also see the famous double star cluster, visible without a telescope. The two clusters are almost twins, and only about 50 light years apart, although over 7,000 light years away.

LYRA

Stars don't stay the same for ever. They can last billions of years, but when they grow old, they change. In Lyra, there's an old star that swelled up into a giant, then puffed off its outside, like a shell, about 7,000 years ago. It formed a nebula called the Ring Nebula around what is left of the old star. You need a telescope to see it.

HERCULES

Some of the oldest stars in our Galaxy can be found in tight, ball-shaped swarms of stars that astronomers call globular clusters. In Hercules you will find the brightest globular cluster in the northern half of the sky. Known simply as M13, it has no other name. About 300,000 stars are packed in this cluster, which is over 20,000 light years away. You can see it without a telescope.

ORION

Glowing gas around a group of bright young stars forms the famous Orion Nebula in the Hunter's sword. Behind the Nebula lurks a huge dark cloud of gas and dust 1,300 light years away. This is a birthplace of stars. No more than a hundred thousand years ago, the stars in the Orion Nebula began to shine, blasting through the dark cloud with their rays and lighting up the gas around them. The Nebula is visible without a telescope.

CENTAURUS

Centaurus is home to the brightest and biggest of all globular star clusters. Called Omega Centauri, it is 16,500 light years away and 620 light years across. You can easily see it without a telescope.

The brightest star in this constellation, Alpha Centauri, is the nearest bright star to the Sun. In reality it is a double star, just over 4 light years away. The two stars slowly waltz around each other once every 80 years. A very dim star in Centaurus, called Proxima, is a tiny bit nearer to us than Alpha.

ARGO

The huge southern constellation Argo Navis (the Ship *Argo*) existed for about 2,000 years. Then, in 1930, it was officially split into three when astronomers agreed to divide up the sky into 88 constellations. The parts of Argo are Carina (the Keel), Puppis (the Stern) and Vela (the Sail). But long before 1930, astronomers had been using these names for the different parts of Argo. The star Canopus, the brightest in Carina, is the second brightest in the whole sky. Also in Carina lies a lovely, brilliant cluster of 30 newly-formed stars, quite different from the old globular clusters. Although the cluster doesn't have a special name, it's easy to see without a telescope.

NORTHERN SKY

This star map has the North Celestial Pole as its centre. It shows constellations of the northern sky. Constellations lying across the celestial equator appear on both maps. Paler areas represent the Milky Way.

Constellations on the map of the northern sky featured in this book:

Andromeda

Cassiopeia

Cepheus

Hercules

Lyra – the Lyre

Ophiuchus

Orion

Pegasus

Perseus

Aquarius

Cetus

Mira

Pegasus

Aries

Eridanus

Delphinus

Andromeda

Triangulum

Taurus

Pleiades

Aquila

Altair

Cygnus

Algol

Perseus

Hyades

Deneb

Aldebaran

Vulpecula

Cassiopeia

Rigel

Serpens
Cauda

Lyra

Cepheus

Capella

Orion

Vega

Polaris

Auriga

Betelgeuse

Hercules

Ursa Minor

Ophiuchus

Draco

Castor

Gemini

Corona
Borealis

Pollux

Ursa
Major

Lynx

Procyon

Boötes

Canes
Venatici

Canis Minor

Serpens Caput

Arcturus

Regulus

Hydra

Libra

Leo

Virgo

Spica

+ marks the Celestial Pole